PETER TRADOWSKY, born in Berlin in 1934, taught at the Rudolf Steiner school in Berlin and co-founded the Waldorf Teacher Training course there. He initiated the building of Rudolf Steiner Haus in Berlin in 1983, and was a key staff member of the Arbeitszentrum (Study Centre) for 21 years until 2005. He is a frequent lecturer, and the author of many books such as *Christ and Antichrist* and *Kaspar Hauser*.

Stigmatization of St Francis (1319–1328) by Giotto, in the Capella Bardi, Chiesa di Santa Croce, Florence

THE STIGMATA

Destiny as a Question of Knowledge

PETER TRADOWSKY

TEMPLE LODGE

Translated from German by Matthew Barton

Temple Lodge Publishing
Hillside House, The Square
Forest Row, RH18 5ES

www.templelodge.com

Published by Temple Lodge 2010

Originally published in German under the title *Stigmatisation* by Verlag am Goetheanum, Dornach, 2009

© Verlag für Anthroposophie, Dornach 2009
This translation © Temple Lodge Publishing 2010

Peter Tradowsky asserts his moral right to be identified as the author of this work

All rights reserved. No part of this publication may be reproduced, stored in a retrieval system, or transmitted, in any form or by any means, electronic, mechanical, photocopying or otherwise, without the prior permission of the publishers

A catalogue record for this book is available from the British Library

ISBN 978 1 906999 13 1

Cover by Andrew Morgan Design featuring a portion of 'St Francis receiving the Stigmata' by El Greco
Typeset by DP Photosetting, Neath, West Glamorgan
Printed and bound by Cromwell Press Group, Trowbridge, Wiltshire

Contents

Preface	1
The Unspoken Name, and Namelessness	3
The Stigmata	6
Continuous Fasting	36
Normative Morals	45
Supposed Authorities	48
Afterword	52
Notes	59

Preface

This little book is a response to an appendix entitled 'The Forces of the Phantom and Stigmatization' from the book by Sergei O. Prokofieff entitled *The Mystery of the Resurrection in the Light of Anthroposophy*.[1] In a very strange way this appendix engages with and confronts Judith von Halle, who received the stigmata at Passiontide 2004. I say 'strange' because the author does not mention her name,[2] yet the reader quickly realizes that Judith von Halle is his sole focus. In this essay by Prokofieff, the stigmata are treated in a way that has little or nothing to do with reality, as I aim to show in this aphoristic account.

Sadly one also discovers that Prokofieff's analysis is badly flawed in logical, methodological and factual respects, and requires correction, as will become apparent.

A correction is required above all because in many places the reader is likely to find it extremely difficult to perceive the errors and flaws in Prokofieff's argument. This would only be possible by carefully examining the more or less obscure sources he draws on, which in practice is hardly feasible. A reader should, however, be able to rely on an author quoting from sources in an academically responsible, careful and objective way. This does not preclude mistakes of course, but should be discernible as a basic stance.

Even when Prokofieff cites Rudolf Steiner, as he often does, the quotations are frequently taken out of context to support his own views, or wholly misinterpreted.

The real problem with Prokofieff's account, however, is not its one-sided and tendentious character, but the fact that it is rooted in a fundamental error that pervades it and is sustained only by excluding important aspects of the whole phenomenon of stigmatization (e.g. continuous fasting). It is therefore necessary to counter the unreality of Prokofieff's presentation with something that starts from reality. Prokofieff's view of stigmatization might well spread a great deal of confusion about this subject. Nor should we overlook the fact that an unfavourable light is cast on the person of Judith von Halle once the reader of the piece realizes the real thrust of this text.

To counter this, the present text aims to look at stigmatization in a more comprehensive and multifaceted way, insofar as it is possible to elucidate its mysterious nature in a short book. At the same time I also wish to oppose the unjustified characterization of the stigmatic Judith von Halle, whom, as we have said, Prokofieff does not mention by name.

Peter Tradowsky
Berlin-Dahlem, March 2009

The Unspoken Name, and Namelessness

Within the Anthroposophical Society and the wider anthroposophical movement, and even amongst a wider public, the question of stigmatization has not in any way been prominent in recent decades. For the study of anthroposophy, stigmatization is certainly a very marginal theme which might awaken a specific interest but cannot otherwise – though probably we should now say could not previously – be regarded as important.

At Passiontide and Easter 2004, Judith von Halle – a colleague at Rudolf Steiner House in Berlin – received the stigmata. Thus, within the Anthroposophical Society, and specifically its Berlin network, a fact of destiny occurred which has continued to call forth responses of various kinds. After about six months, from the autumn of 2004 therefore, Judith von Halle decided to speak about her experiences, and her presentations were from the very beginning imbued with and cognizant of Rudolf Steiner's spiritual-scientific findings. Her lectures on this theme appeared as a book entitled *And If He Has Not Been Raised*... (the English translation appeared in 2007). They spoke to a wide circle of people but also – primarily subliminally – evoked dismissal and resistance. The leading councils and committees of the Anthroposophical Society in Germany and in Dornach were unable to respond to Judith von Halle and her intentions in a positive and open-minded way. Ultimately this led to Judith von Halle and those connected with her being dismissed from Rudolf Steiner House in Berlin in August 2005. Thus, without any valid reasons, circumstances arose that from then on caused disastrous effects within the Anthroposophical Society. Within the anthroposophical community, the best one can say is that people have continued to work parallel to, but not with, one another. Little or nothing has so far occurred in the Anthroposophical Society to resolve this dilemma.

In December 2008, Sergei Prokofieff published the original German edition of *The Mystery of the Resurrection in the Light of Anthroposophy*, which included the appendix 'The Forces of the Phantom and Stigmatization'. The whole book, not just the appendix, is a committed examination of the destiny and work of Judith von Halle, but the reader will seek there in vain for a mention of her name. Within the Anthroposophical Society the theme of the stigmata is only worth mentioning in consequence of Judith von Halle; the reader will and is also meant to realize this, yet Prokofieff uses a kind of mystification which, in the circumstances, conceals nothing. Basically he does not address stigmatization in general but only one person with the stigmata, yet leaves her nameless, and proceeds against her in a fiercely radical and almost destructive way. It has sometimes been said that not mentioning a name can act as a kind of protection. Here though, the unmistakeable reference to Judith von Halle renders such protection illusory.

Whatever the reasons may be that moved Prokofieff to omit Judith von Halle's name, he has to accept censure for something that is totally unacceptable in literary terms.

Worse still is that Prokofieff cites the expression 'travelling back in time' – used otherwise only by Judith von Halle – without naming his source, which is an elementary obligation both academically and humanely.

It is also tantamount to an insult when Prokofieff reduces the human being Judith von Halle to someone whose stigmata is her only feature, whereas of course she possesses substantial other capacities, primarily those of working in a spiritual-scientific way and presenting her findings, which she has done in a series of publications. These seem not to exist for Prokofieff. Except for her first book, her publications have nothing to do with her stigmata, and arise only from her capacity for spiritual-scientific work.

Is it humane or considerate to render a human being nameless, concealing her behind figures such as Anne Catherine Emmerich[3] or Therese Neumann (of Konnersreuth) – who after all play no part within the Anthroposophical Society or in a contemporary context? Intentionally passing over a real human being amounts to lack of respect for this individual, which is irreconcilable with human dignity.

The Stigmata

The very first sentence in the appendix of Prokofieff's book betrays his outlook: he speaks there of 'the phenomenon of what is known as stigmatization as frequently encountered in the history of the Roman Catholic Church'.[4] The phrase 'what is known as' aims to suggest immediately to readers that there is, or ought to be, really no such thing as the stigmata, especially since it is connected with the Roman Catholic Church. Does this mean that a possible rejection of the Catholic Church is also extended to the stigmata? At any rate, from the outset there is no sign here of an objective and unprejudiced stance towards the stigmata.

Prokofieff's whole portrayal of stigmatization rests on a fundamental error: without stating, and thus explaining his stance, he starts from the assumption that the stigmata are self-induced by the person who receives them, and that the same person can also get rid of them again. For Prokofieff, the stigmata represent a failed and above all unreliable path towards Christian initiation. This is however nothing other than a construct created by Prokofieff himself, against which he proceeds with fervour, as it were with fire and sword, without noticing that his account has nothing whatever to do with the destiny of those who receive the stigmata. Underlying this outlook is the long outdated and refuted assumption that the stigmata are caused by suggestion and autosuggestion. The decisive flaw in this context is his failure to engage with the stigmata phenomenon and the biographical reality of those who experience it.

Stigmatization occurs suddenly and without prior announcement as a fact of destiny. It differs from other strokes of destiny by its extraordinary nature and the way it takes hold of a person's whole life, but in principle this is an event that occurs involuntarily, without intention or conscious participation. Like all strokes of destiny, stigmatization is received from without, as if from a wider sphere, and it is therefore pointless to ask whether it is true or false. A fact of destiny is just that, and can only be accepted as such. In one's present life at least, such facts do not proceed from a free decision, but arise through karma. Karma, however, in particular as it relates to the physical body, is caused by the first hierarchy.

If stigmatization is understood as individual karma, then it is impossible to regard it as the result of some kind of asceticism, schooling or even research. Never has it been claimed that stigmatization is the goal of any path of schooling. This is confirmed if one studies the biographies of those who received the stigmata, who in no way prepared themselves for this destined event.

This does not mean, of course, that the greater I living in the higher consciousness of the world of spirit has not been working intentionally towards such a destined event. Awareness of this can indeed arise in retrospect.

In epistemological terms, the experiences of those who receive the stigmata clearly belong to the aspect of perception,[5] throwing up questions of interpretation and knowledge but not themselves offering knowledge as such. Prokofieff can only arrive at his fundamental error by entirely overlooking the 'percept side' of things and, astonishingly, the difference between perceptions and thinking. One can see this in particularly gross form in the following passage:

> However, for an anthroposophist one thing is absolutely clear: *all this has nothing to do with anthroposophy and its*

spiritual-scientific research! And if such somnambulistic 'methods of research' enter into anthroposophy and become widespread within it, this would mean the abandonment of the spiritual-scientific method of research and hence, the end of anthroposophy as spiritual science.[6]

Not only is this a misunderstanding in relation to stigmatization but also a complete failure to acknowledge the experiences that arise through it. Nowhere is it clearer that Prokofieff is battling against constructs he himself has created, for, in truth, the experiences of those who receive the stigmata have as little to do with anthroposophy as any other perceptions. They can, though, become the subject of spiritual-scientific research and can be investigated using spiritual-scientific means and methods: they are a task for, and not the result of, spiritual science.

All statements which relate stigmatization to the practice of a Christian path of initiation are thus unfounded, and will not be discussed further here.

It is noticeable that Prokofieff primarily refers to Anne Catherine Emmerich, and far less to Therese of Konnersreuth. Could this be due to the fact that Anne Catherine Emmerich's comments were recorded by Clemens Brentano who, as a poet converted to Catholicism, undoubtedly lent his accounts the tone of would-be Catholic piety – and therefore never reproduces the original tenor of what she said? This at least enables Prokofieff to stress his thesis that stigmatization is a specifically Catholic phenomenon, and for this reason alone should be dismissed.

If Prokofieff had paid greater attention to Therese of Konnersreuth (8 April 1898 – 18 September 1962) he would have discovered comprehensive accounts that – though some of them, certainly, are controversial – describe and document facts about Therese in a way lacking for Anne Catherine Emmerich (since modern investigative methods were not yet available in her case). Accounts by both friends and enemies of Therese cannot solve the questions surrounding her, but they do offer a wide field of observation. It is a mystery why Prokofieff does not cite these records, or at least the informative book by Luise Rinser published in 1954 entitled *Die Wahrheit über Konnersreuth* ('The Truth about Konnersreuth'). Based on the author's own experiences with Therese of Konnersreuth, this compiles the main findings and investigations relating to her.

Those who receive the stigmata – and this is true also of Judith von Halle – seem fated to invoke a fierce response both for and against them.[7] Only a sober and respectful examination of the phenomena is likely to be able to overcome this strong tug in either a negative or positive direction. What occurred in the Anthroposophical Society in relation to Judith von Halle was similar to the Catholic Church's reaction to Therese of Konnersreuth. Sadly, no substantial difference is noticeable.

Initially one can remark a profound sense of shock or – as with Prokofieff – a fierce rejection, both of which have marked irrational traits and betray the consternation of soul that can arise in response to an inability to grasp what is indeed an extraordinary experience.

In the current case, Prokofieff does not appear to have taken Rudolf Steiner's methodology to heart. This consists of making as full a picture as possible of a being or set of circumstances by studying scientific or other accounts relating to them. He has paid no attention to non-anthroposophical literature here, or at least he does not cite non-anthroposophical authors. By proceeding like this, Prokofieff's conclusions lack a relation to reality.

The destinies of those who receive the stigmata present us with two serious questions of knowledge:
1. What underlying destiny leads to stigmatization at a particular point in a person's life? Or, to put this in the terms of spiritual science: what individual karma gives rise to stigmatization? And what capacities are connected with it?
2. How does stigmatization arise? How can it be explained? And what significance does it have?

Let me say straight away that I do not claim to be able to solve these questions finally here; but I do want to try to clarify the questions themselves and offer some thoughts that may help to resolve them. I also want to stress that what I have to say relates to the particular person who is the focus of this book. These thoughts could only be applied to other people who receive the stigmata following careful investigation, since the word 'stigmata' itself includes a wide range of possible phenomena.

In relation to the first question it is important to remember that, according to both academic and spiritual-scientific findings, the Mystery of Golgotha occurred on the physical plane on 3 April in the year 33. This fact also implies that there were witnesses to this event: people, in other words, whose karma it was to encounter Christ in earthly existence. The Gospels also speak of this, but there are no other historical testimonies of Christ's life and sufferings in Palestine. The Mystery of Golgotha is an earthly event which, as striving human beings, we can recognize as a spiritual fact. It can lead to our encounter, as it first did for Paul, with the living, present Christ.

Stigmatics experience, in an altered state of awareness, and usually on Fridays or Sundays, that they are involuntarily

The Stigmata 11

transported back to the events at Golgotha as if they were contemporary witnesses of it. Whether the expression 'somnambulatory' is fitting to describe this state of awareness is less important than the fact that a stigmatic's experience is immediate and as present as a memory. A past that is unchanged is exactly repeated in the present. How this comes about is an open question, and we know of no comment by Rudolf Steiner that refers to it.

That sensory perceptions are not involved was shown by the scientifically dubious and humanely disrespectful blind trials on Therese of Konnersreuth, which demonstrated, in what can only be described as a brutal manner, that her senses were not involved. A reality once experienced, which is retained as a memory, can surface again vividly. Let me use two examples to clarify what I mean.

Judith von Halle reports that she hears Christ's words from the cross as 'Eloi, Eloi, l'ma shevachtani!'[8] In Matthew (27, 46) these words are given (in the King James version) as 'Eli, Eli, lama sabachthani', and in Mark (15, 34) as 'Eloi, Eloi, lama sabachthani', then, on both occasions immediately translated as 'My God, my God, why hast thou forsaken me?' Rudolf Steiner quotes these decisive words,[9] but translates them differently. He renders them as the words of initiation which the adept spoke after a mystery sleep:

> By speaking thus of the world of spirit, a person proclaims the spirit within the physical world, and becomes a missionary of the spirit. And this is expressed in the words, 'Eli, Eli, lama sabachthani!' This means: My God, my God, how you have glorified me! This was what one could originally hear from the mouth of every person who was initiated in this way.[10]

Somewhat later Rudolf Steiner clarifies these words further

as: 'My God, my God, how you have glorified, spiritualized the I in humanity,' and states: 'That is what these words mean.'[11] Rudolf Steiner can determine this true content of Christ's words from his reading of the Akashic records. Judith von Halle initially points out that 'sabachthani' is correctly translated as 'forsaken'. But since she is aware of, and takes seriously, the results of Rudolf Steiner's spiritual research, she knows that ultimately there can be no contradiction between the Akashic records and observations on the physical plane: experiences on both this side and the other side of the threshold must accord with each other. The decisive word which she hears differently is 'shevachtani', which does indeed mean raised, glorified, spiritualized. From her knowledge of Hebrew and Aramaic language and script she is also able to show how the word 'sabachthani' came about, meaning 'forsaken'. Spoken by Christ on the cross, both meanings make sense simultaneously, insofar as the human being Jesus on the cross experiences how humanity has left the world of spirit, and is forsaken by it.

Three capacities combine in Judith von Halle: through her stigmatization she can hear the precise words of Christ on the cross; through her knowledge of Rudolf Steiner's research she can recognize that his reading of the Akashic records enabled him to perceive the content of Christ's words in contrast to the traditional version; and through her knowledge of Hebrew (Aramaic) language and script she can tell us how the false version could arise, also due to lack of familiarity with initiation practices.

Thus in Judith von Halle we have a concordance of hearing, recognition and knowledge of language, which finally offers a satisfactory explanation of a passage in the Gospels that hitherto has been hard to understand. All Christians, insofar as they become aware of the meaning of Christ's words, should thank her from the bottom of their hearts for managing to resolve the apparent contradictions here.

Something similar can be found in the case of Therese of Konnersreuth. In her 'ecstatic state' she heard and spoke Aramaic, which she certainly could not have encountered in her ordinary life. Therese was so certain of what she heard that she disputed about the precise words with a scholar who tried to correct her:

> Thus Therese, for example, claimed that in her ecstatic state she had heard Christ on the cross say: 'Es-che' ('I thirst'). Professor Wutz countered that it should be 'sachana'. Despite his thorough knowledge of Aramaic, he had never heard 'es-che'. But Therese insisted she was correct. She had heard what she heard. And indeed, she was right! After careful philological study, it was found that this phrase did indeed exist, and that it was the commonly used expression rather than 'sachana'.[12]

These and other examples show experiences that are not merely subjective but are precisely described perceptions which, as suggested, bear the character of memory.

A particular question relates to the form of the cross on which Christ was crucified. Three stigmatics (Anne Catherine Emmerich, Therese Neumann and Judith von Halle) state that they perceive the cross as Y-shaped.[13] The very slight divergences here correspond with what one might expect of different people's observations and ways of presenting things in ordinary life. But Prokofieff now tries to refute the correctness of these perceptions, although it is fundamentally impossible to decide the content of a perception through thinking. Let us recall Rudolf Steiner's own example in relation to a whale: it cannot logically be proven whether a whale exists or not, but can only be ascertained through perception.[14] Prokofieff however asserts that Rudolf Steiner's research shows the cross on Golgotha had the normal cross-form – without however offering any evidence from Steiner's collected works to back this up, which he otherwise never omits to do. That Rudolf Steiner used and cited the normal form of the cross does not necessarily have any relevance to its historical shape. Stigmatics' perceptions can be doubted, but it cannot be proven that they are wrong. Nor is this possible by citing Christian history, as Prokofieff does. But for him this supplies firm evidence, as shown by his sentence: 'It seems fairly obvious that, although she [Anne Catherine Emmerich] beheld her sightings with her physical eyes, she must nevertheless have seen incorrectly.'[15]

What is quite certain is that stigmatics do not see their vision in sensory form, just as little as we perceive memories by sensory perception. The processes of perception described above draw on a different consciousness than that of sensory vision. It is also unclear why and how Prokofieff believes she has 'seen incorrectly' with sensory vision. Goethe says: 'In the senses you can trust, for they will never lead you false'; and goes on to conclude: 'Not the senses but the judgement errs.' Why should Anne Catherine Emmerich and the other stigmatics, who all knew the usual shape of the cross, say something different if it does not correspond with their perceptions?[16]

In another context, too, it is clear how thinking is being used. Prokofieff reports that Rudolf Steiner created the three models of Christ's head with his own hands: 'This is attested by the two photographs showing him at work.'[17] Prokofieff may of course be right, but with the best will in the world these photographs cannot prove it.

As we noted, Judith von Halle uses the phrase 'travelling back in time' for her experience of historical events at the time

The Stigmata   15

of Christ. The phrase is apt for conveying part of the process that unfolds in a different state of consciousness, that is, being transposed to an era nearly two millennia in the past. This shift occurs involuntarily, especially at particular times on Fridays, Saturdays and Sundays. If we understand the words 'travel' as a journey that is intentionally undertaken, this is misleading since she does not voluntarily embark on this 'time travel' or make a conscious decision to do so.

In this other state of consciousness, stigmatics can also perceive events that are not directly connected with the Mystery of Golgotha, such as the Jordan baptism. They can also move about within these perceived events, which suggests that they are not merely memories. Access to such experiences is however always via the point of departure and focus of the Mystery of Golgotha and an intense relationship with the being of Christ.

Naturally we can ask how we should evaluate stigmatics' experiences. I would like to point here to a possibly related observation. Rudolf Steiner's *Calendar of the Soul* begins with Easter Sunday, whose date changes from year to year. The annual stream of time describes a lemniscate, returning after a year to Easter Sunday as the day of Resurrection. From Christ's Resurrection on the original Easter Sunday, a stream of life flows like a spiritual wave or current, enlivening the human being and the earth even if we scarcely notice this. This process recurs each year, but is only possible because the events of Good Friday likewise recur. It is self-evident that Good Friday and Easter Sunday belong together inseparably. At Passiontide is prepared the process which matures in Holy Week, leading in a transformation and metamorphosis to the Resurrection impetus, by means of which Christ once again blesses humanity and the earth with life and vitality. This process likewise recurs each week in miniature between

Friday and Sunday, not of course with the same intensity as for the whole year but adapted to the rhythm of the week. There are certainly people who can experience these processes more or less clearly at the margins of their awareness, in much diluted form.

Through their profound connection with the Mystery of Golgotha, stigmatics experience this life stream emanating from Christ with elemental intensity. Their destiny draws them into this life stream and embeds them in it. This helps us understand, at least a little, the nature of stigmatics' lives. This is not a spiritual-scientific research finding, but an attempt to deepen our understanding.

The precise recall detailed above might easily suggest that stigmatics are people who lived in close proximity to Jesus Christ in Palestine in a previous life. This thought occurs to Luise Rinser when she says: 'Therese was not present at the scenes of Christ's Passion, unless one assumes reincarnation.'[18] If we consider that in the two thousand years of Christianity only a tiny number of people have received the stigmata, we realize that – if this idea is right – special circumstances must have obtained at their incarnation at the time of Christ which led to them becoming stigmatics later. However small the original community of Christians was, it was certainly much larger than the number of known stigmatics.

We must also reflect that things are recalled which could not have been experienced directly. A particularly striking example of this is the account which Rudolf Steiner gives of Peter. It should be expressly stated that the word 'memory' itself does not imply anything either for or against the reincarnation of someone who was present at the time. But in the context given here, it is significant that 'sensory, physical' events are 'recalled' that the person himself did not experience. Rudolf Steiner states:

The Stigmata   17

Although the Mystery of Golgotha took place on the physical plane, one can approach it only by clairvoyant means. We have to remember this. The Gospels indicate this clearly when they state that at the decisive moment the most committed disciples had fled. Thus in a soul such as that of Peter, once this soul received the impulse of the Resurrected Christ, a memory surfaced of what had occurred after his flight. Usually we recall only what we witness directly in sensory existence. But the kind of clairvoyance which arose amongst the disciples contrasts with normal recall in that one remembers physical, sensory events at which one was not present. In relation to the surfacing of memory in such a soul as that of Peter, we must therefore think of events this soul did not directly witness. And thus to those who wished to hear him, Peter taught about the Mystery of Golgotha 'by memory': he taught his pupils what he remembered, despite not having been present.[19]

As probable as it may seem to think that stigmatization is connected with having lived at the time of Christ, this would need confirming through serious, precise spiritual research, which would be the only way to clarify the karmic background of someone who receives the stigmata. Here one could envisage both general karmic conditions that might lead to stigmatization, and also individual circumstances of a karmic nature.

If we recognize that stigmatization phenomena are due to as yet unknown karmic reasons, this underlines the fact that stigmatization can never be the result or goal of exercises or schooling in a current life.

This also allows us to understand that most Christian saints and others connected with Christ do not receive the stigmata, presumably because these specific karmic conditions are not present and therefore of course cannot as it were be recreated.

We need to remember that sense-free thinking has not so far led to intuitions that might help clarify the question of knowledge posed here.

Prokofieff tries to derive his account of the stigmata from a remark Rudolf Steiner made in response to a question about Clemens Brentano's descriptions of Anne Catherine Emmerich: 'The sightings recorded here are of an exceptionally good somnambulist. Especially the parts which relate to mirror-vision have without any doubt something extraordinarily right about them.'[20] It is however worth noting that this comment by Steiner about a stigmatic, the only one we know of, has so far not been published by the editors of Rudolf Steiner's complete works, probably because they were not sure about its provenance. Despite this, Prokofieff bases his argument, and above all his negative judgement of stigmatization, on this single passage.

Anne Catherine Emmerich's 'visions' are certainly not sensory perceptions, as Prokofieff suggests, and this is clearly demonstrated by the blind trials on Therese of Konnersreuth which were mentioned above. The altered state of consciousness excludes sensory perception, even if it involves experiences, as though in a closed room, which seem to resemble memories of sensory perceptions. Memories of perceptions can of course be extraordinarily intense.

Since the expression 'mirrored vision' does not appear anywhere in the collected works – which was no doubt also why its editors did not include the sentences about Anne Catherine Emmerich in their volumes – Prokofieff tries to relate Rudolf Steiner's accounts of somnambulism to the stigmatic Anne Catherine Emmerich, accentuating that the basis for somnambulism is 'always a sick or enfeebled life of soul'.[21] It is clear where this is tending: the stigmatic and somnambulist Anne Catherine Emmerich had a 'sick or enfeebled life of soul', and therefore this applies to all stigmatics, and thus also to the person who is really the focus of these deliberations, Judith von Halle.

Prokofieff does not appear to notice the contradictions between his statement above that 'she must have seen incorrectly' and Rudolf Steiner's indication that Emmerich's sightings 'have without any doubt something extraordinarily right about them'. It remains to be clarified where error or truth arise, and for what reasons. The fact remains, though, that there are no reliable comments in Rudolf Steiner's works relating to stigmatization and stigmatics.

The unfounded view proposed by Prokofieff that stigmatization is not a matter of destiny but a voluntarily induced phenomenon, which one can therefore also 'remedy', amounts to latent discrimination against all stigmatics which – as we will see – Prokofieff also applies to Saint Francis. This latent discrimination can be countered by saying that Anne Catherine Emmerich and Therese Neumann came from simple backgrounds and had a poor level of education. They were good people who bravely bore their difficult fate and we can generously acknowledge them as such. It is particularly concerning to see their Catholic faith being used as some kind of reproach against them. They were born into Catholic families and there was certainly no reason why they should develop an impetus, in this life, to distance themselves from their faith community.

By receiving the stigmata, Therese of Konnersreuth also acquired faculties which she did not previously have and which distinguish her in a special way:

> The fact that Therese uses her mystic gifts of prophesy, intuitive heart knowledge and good advice exclusively for positive ends, and that ultimately only good was done by

her, can allow us to believe that the *causa prima* of these gifts ... is the inexplicable: God himself.[22]

These gifts are well substantiated by numerous and in some instances astonishing examples. Over and above this, Therese had the capacity to suffer in place of another, that is, to take upon herself redemptive suffering to heal or alleviate another's illness. She could intentionally relieve a person of his illness, but only by suffering physically and psychologically herself. She later helped sick children in this way, to the extent that her capacity for suffering allowed this. Naturally Therese had not heard of the idea of karma, but she intervened benevolently in the karma of sick people, no doubt aware that such help is only effective through giving actual aid – and not only through physical suffering.

In the state of 'elevated composure' – as Therese's special state of consciousness was called, as opposed to 'ecstasy' – she was capable of special insights:

> She was once asked who the first stigmatic had been and she answered that it was Paul; however he had not borne the stigmata upon but within his body – a suggestion which theological exegesis of relevant passages in Paul's letters proved to be correct.[23]

In this state of 'elevated composure' she could also become a medium in the sense of being the servant of a spiritual being, and was fully aware of this fact. She declared, for example, that in this condition,

> it is not her giving information, but Christ (or her guardian angel or a saint) is speaking through her. She in no way identifies herself with Christ, but knows herself only to be a medium of whom Christ makes use. Since, as we know from the character and disposition of her personality, she

has an unusual capacity to place herself into the background for the sake of the central idea at work in her life, it is fully possible for her to extinguish herself entirely in the state of elevated composure, and to be nothing but a medium.[24]

As medium she was fully aware of the division between her person and her task of allowing spiritual things to speak through her.

Whether this special state of consciousness can properly be called 'somnambulist' is questionable since past things are not uttered in it, but spiritual entities respond to current questions or problems.

It is particularly astonishing that Therese of Konnersreuth had clear foresight about the Third Reich: in January 1933 she said: ' "Do not try, for you will never learn anything about this. You know already that things won't end well." This was one of Therese's few predictions about the Third Reich.'[25] Therese said nothing about the source of her knowledge, but it was the source of truth. She refrained from external prognoses.

She did however use her capacity for foresight to warn persecuted people and show them a means to avoid danger, even telling this or that person of an escape route they could take.

These remarks are intended to redress the honour of Therese of Konnersreuth and also, in some sense, of Anne Catherine Emmerich.

The question above about the occurrence of stigmatization and its possible explanation requires us to consider the biographical and physical conditions associated with it. 'Therese has borne the stigmata since 1926, and – like all mystic gifts – she received them suddenly and unexpectedly.'[26] This highlights an important biographical feature of the stigmata: as mentioned at the beginning, they appear without any prior inkling or intent, and do not announce themselves in advance in any way. Initially they show as little connection with the person's biography as any other event that occurs as an unexpected stroke of destiny, the reason for which can only subsequently be understood. Overlooking this fact is what leads to Prokofieff's fundamental error. Even if stigmatics share in the experience of the Resurrection, their lives are full of pain and suffering, and they are subject to enmity and antagonism from their surrounding communities. It is very unlikely that anyone would ever consciously choose such a fate. Stigmatization can only proceed from a much deeper stratum of awareness in which we live within the powers of destiny – that is, with our will, of which we ourselves are unconscious, within the beings of the spiritual world that form human destiny in accordance with the laws of karma. Strokes of destiny are inconceivable without the will of the spiritual world. This is particularly true of an event as incisive as that of stigmatization. Why should we not be open-minded enough to accept this?

Stigmata that appear suddenly and involuntarily are clearly defined by medicine. They are self-forming wounds without external cause which do not become infected or inflamed, but do not heal either. They are therefore different from all other types of wound. They cannot be removed, either, by brutal methods such as cauterization with a branding iron. At certain moments, the stigmata exude a little or more blood. Despite careful monitoring of these phenomena, no medical explanation has so far been found.

Prokofieff, who apparently has not given the subject any deeper study, regards the stigmata as intrinsically suspicious because they are corporeal signs, and in his view represent a false path. In support of this view he seems to act as a prosecution witness on behalf of Rudolf Steiner, claiming that this was why the latter never referred to the stigmatization of Francis of Assisi. Francis received in his astral body an image of the astral body of Jesus Christ:

> This – and not the stigmata – was for Rudolf Steiner what was most characteristic about St. Francis ... It was not the appearance of the bodily wounds but the high moral strength which he possessed through bearing a likeness of Jesus's astral body that was of central significance for Rudolf Steiner.[27]

There is a clear undertone in these sentences: Rudolf Steiner does not mention the stigmata because they are of little moral value. But this is Prokofieff's view! It is pure speculation on his part that Rudolf Steiner shared his opinion. It remains an open question why Rudolf Steiner says nothing demonstrable about Francis of Assisi's stigmata, or about the stigmata in general, in his collected works. It may simply be because there was no cause to do so during his lifetime, since Therese of Neumann's stigmata only appeared in 1926.

Prokofieff's dubious stance towards the stigmata of Francis of Assisi also surfaces in the former's strange remark that the stigmata 'appeared only two years before his death'.[28] What is he really saying here? That Francis only had to bear the misfortune of the stigmata for two years? Or something else? Here, as in many other passages, Prokofieff's method of subliminally influencing the reader is all too clear.

In historical or biographical terms, however, Prokofieff's statement that Francis of Assisi concealed the stigmata so carefully that they were only discovered on his corpse after death[29] is untenable. Below I will counter these claims with historical testimonies.

In the monumental work by Henry Thode on Francis of Assisi and the beginnings of Renaissance art in Italy,[30] there is an appendix with a detailed account of all the circumstances and facts surrounding his stigmatization, which I draw on here, and which entirely contradicts Prokofieff's version. The very first sentence already makes this clear: 'In this part we will most reverently consider the glorious and sacred wounds of our blessed father St Francis, which he received from Christ upon the holy mountain of La Vernia.'[31] The sources tell in clear stages how the stigmata were received, and how Francis was in a certain sense prepared for them shortly before:

> On the day preceding the festival of the raising of the Cross, in the month of September, as St Francis was closeted in his cell and praying, the angel of God appeared to him and said to him in God's name: 'I urge you and warn you to prepare yourself humbly, and ready yourself to accept in all patience what God will wish to do to you and give you.' St Francis replied: 'I am ready to bear patiently all that the Lord will do unto me.' And after he had spoken thus, the angel vanished.[32]

The following day, that of the festival of the raising of the Cross, St Francis humbled himself in prayer and asked that he might feel, in this life still, the most bitter Passion of Christ and the boundlessness of his love. Finally he understood that God would hear him:

> As St Francis became inwardly aware of this promise, he began in the most profound reverence to consider the sufferings of Christ; and the fervour of his reverence grew within him so that from pure love and compassion he was transformed entirely into Jesus. And, kindled and enflamed with these thoughts, he saw the same morning a seraph

descend from the heavens with six bright and fiery wings, and approaching him with such swift speed that he bore the form of a crucified man; and his wings were such that two wings spread out above his head, two were spread for flight and two more encompassed his body. When St Francis saw this, he was mightily afraid and was at the same time filled with joy, pain and astonishment. He had great joy in Christ's sweet gaze which regarded him with such familiarity and grace; yet as he perceived him hanging upon the Cross, he felt the immeasurable pain of sympathy.

As Francis was having this experience, the mountain of La Vernia was wreathed in flames and light so that the people thought day had already dawned. Francis, however, was receiving the stigmata:

> But now, after that wonderful vision [the seraph] had vanished after a fair space of time, and after secret speech, it left in St Francis's heart a mighty burning and the flames of divine love; and upon his flesh it left a wondrous trace and image of the Passion of Christ: for upon his hands and feet the marks of the nails appeared, as he had seen these in the body of Jesus Christ, the Crucified One, who appeared to him in the form of the seraph. And thus his hands and feet appeared as if penetrated by nails, the heads of which were on the palms of his hands and soles of his feet... Similarly there appeared on his right side the image of an unhealed lance wound, red and bleeding, from which oftentimes blood would pour thereafter, so that his habit and the clothing upon his legs grew red.[34]

This account shows plainly – as all stigmatics have experienced in one way or another – that it is impossible to conceal the stigmata as Prokofieff wrongly claims. The passage continues:

And so his followers noticed before he himself spoke word of it that he kept his hands hidden and likewise his feet, and that he was unable to place his feet upon the ground; then they also found that his habit showed blood and the clothing on his legs when they washed it; and they grasped that he bore the image and marks of our Lord Jesus Christ imprinted on hands and feet and likewise on his side.[35]

It is clear that St Francis tried to conceal the wounds but that this was not possible in the close community with his brothers. He also asked himself,

> whether he should not tell them of the seraphic vision, and how he had received the sacred wounds.
>
> Finally, since he was plagued with the thorn of his conscience, he called to him some of his most trusted brothers and presented to them his doubts in general words, without explicitly referring to the circumstances, and asked them for their counsel. But there was one among those brothers of great sanctity, named Brother Illuminato. Truly illumined by God, the latter understood that St Francis must have had vision of wondrous things, and spoke to him thus: 'Brother Francis, know that God will sometimes show his mysteries to you for the sake of others, and not for you alone; you must surely have good reason to fear that you might do great wrong if you conceal what God revealed to you for the benefit of others.' These words persuaded St Francis to relate, with great hesitancy, the whole circumstances and vision, and to add that Christ, who had appeared to him, had proclaimed to him things which he wished never to speak of so long as he lived.[36]

This highlights the conflict of conscience that all stigmatics suffer, not least – though under quite different circumstances

– Judith von Halle. The first recorded stigmatic thus underwent in exemplary fashion all the difficulties which arise for all stigmatics.

For the rest of his life, it is true, St Francis did not speak of certain things, but after his death he revealed the words that Christ spoke to him in that seraphic vision:

> 'Do you know,' asked Christ 'what I have done unto you? I have given you the wound marks which are the signs of my Passion, so that you may bear my banner. And as I descended to the gates of hell on the day of my death, and all souls whom I found there led upwards by the power of these, my wounds, so I grant you that each year, on the day of your death, you descend to purgatory and lead forth all souls of your three orders ... and also the others, wherever you may find them, who honoured you greatly; and by the power of your wounds lead them into the glory of paradise, so that in death you are like unto me, as you were like unto me in life.[37]

According to this testimony, Francis of Assisi and those around him regarded his stigmatization as an intervention by Christ in his life and that of his associates. In this account, it is Francis himself who describes how he received the stigmata; and this description was clearly the basis for several paintings which – particularly in relation to the stigmatization – fairly faithfully follow Francis's words. The best known of these pictures is no doubt the fresco by Giotto in the Bardi chapel at the church of Santa Croce in Florence. But in Assisi, too, there is a Giotto fresco which portrays the stigmatization of Saint Francis.

Prokofieff does not refer at all to these accounts in words, and subsequently in pictures, of Saint Francis's stigmatization; for him they seem not to exist, although they must surely be taken seriously. It is likely that Prokofieff overlooks all this because it would be extremely difficult for him to repudiate these accounts, which refer, after all, to Saint Francis. But he would have to do so if he wished to back up his view about stigmatization.

In fact it is perfectly possible to interpret these medieval accounts of stigmatization through spiritual science. To do so, one has to be clear that stigmatization can arise both within, as it were, through the path of schooling, and from without, as a stroke of destiny: two processes which are markedly different.

In relation to the formation of the inner stigmata, Rudolf Steiner said tellingly:

> But when we begin to feel this right into our physical body – the feet as though bathed in water, the body as though covered in wounds – then we have driven these sensations deeper into our nature so that they penetrate as far as the physical body. They do really penetrate as far as the physical body; for the stigmata appear: the places, steeped in blood, of the wounds of Christ. This means that we drive sensations right into the physical body and know that they can unfold their force even in the body itself; and therefore know that we can feel ourselves grasped more entirely by our being than merely in astral body or etheric body. This can be chiefly characterized as a process in which mystical feelings and sensations work right into our physical body. If we do this, we do nothing other than prepare ourselves in our physical body to gradually receive the phantom that emanates from the grave at Golgotha. We work into our physical body in order to enliven it to such an extent that it feels a relatedness with and attraction for the phantom that arose from the grave at Golgotha.[38]

For the context relevant here, let me first accentuate that the phantom, as the reconfigured archetypal figure of the physical body, bears the stigmata in itself, in the form in which the Resurrected Christ showed himself to the disciples (John, 20, 20 and 27; Luke 24, 39). The Resurrected Christ was portrayed with the stigmata in paintings based on these accounts. There is therefore a clear connection between the phantom and the stigmata. On the path of Christian practice and schooling it is possible, through intense 'I'-work right into the physical body, to draw the phantom towards one as the new Adam. The word 'draw' has a dual meaning here in German ('anziehen' means both 'draw' and 'dress'), also indicating that one creates a new sheath like changing clothes. That this new condition has arisen to some extent becomes manifest through the stigmata, the 'places, steeped in blood, of the wounds of Christ'. These are not bleeding wounds, but places that express the most intensive practice; and it is to be expected that they only appear during spiritual practice and are otherwise concealed. This could be called concealed stigmatization, of which Paul – as mentioned above – was the first witness. The extent to which an individual may have progressed on the path of practice and schooling is his own inmost, sacred concern, as is the question about who has received concealed stigmatization. It is of course decisive here that this 'I'-work, like all paths of practice and schooling, can only be accomplished through someone's free resolve – in other words is voluntary. But at the same time it must never be forgotten that the phantom can only ever be 'received', and therefore always comes like grace from the world of spirit.

The freely chosen nature of the path of schooling contrasts radically with the involuntary nature of stigmatization as a stroke of destiny, as do the more or less bleeding wounds of the stigmata with the less apparent, concealed marks. This is the contrast of inner and outer: stigmatization occurs like sudden fate, as described at the outset, surprising someone suddenly from without. It seems likely, and illuminating to consider, that both the concealed and the palpable stigmata have their common basis in receiving of the phantom. But we should again recall here that stigmatization is extremely rare and can only be understood as particular and very individual karma.

Even if the view described here is not the result of spiritual-scientific research, it is based on an account by Saint Francis who must surely be regarded as a credible and truthful witness. He describes his stigmatization – cited above – as caused by a seraph enclosing the Crucified One. From the latter emanate the rays which call forth the stigmata on the body of Saint Francis, as Giotto painted this scene. Francis experiences his stigmatization as an event that approaches him from without. If doubt were to be cast on this account, it would have to be shown that Saint Francis wrongly described his stigmatization or that he was in error; but, given the particular nature of Saint Francis, such an attempt would inevitably fail.

The view of stigmatization presented here is nothing other than an application of spiritual-scientific findings to the account by Saint Francis. Rudolf Steiner's insight into the phantom as the archetypal form of the physical body reconfigured by the Resurrection was of course not something Saint Francis was aware of; but his description of the seraph enclosing the Crucified One can be seen as a prior form of that. The fact that Saint Francis ascribes his stigmatization to the seraph enclosing the Crucified Christ corresponds to spiritual-scientific knowledge that such intervention into the human being's physical and material body can only be caused by the highest hierarchy, and thus by a seraph. Saint Francis's report is therefore in full accord with spiritual science, if one takes into account the progress in knowledge which spiritual science represents.

It should be stressed that the *one* phantom of Christ, given by Him and received by the human being, multiplies and is individualized – in other words, that the One is common to all and yet individual. This is the growing physical basis for individual freedom despite the generality of the world of ideas or of spirit. That the phantom can only gradually be received in stages is clear to anyone who perceives the reconfiguration of the whole of human nature. Thus this developmental process can only be accomplished through reincarnation; the 'incorruptible body' received directly by the phantom remains available to us from one earthly life to the next.

The following comment by Rudolf Steiner's is of fundamental importance for all striving for knowledge:

> Through what a human being today can undergo as initiation ... a bond of attraction is created between him, insofar as he is incarnated in a physical body, and what was resurrected from the grave at Golgotha as the true archetype of the physical body.[39]

This means, in other words, that abstract thinking by the decadent brain of the old Adam must be succeeded and redeemed by a new, living thinking increasingly founded on the brain of the phantom. True advances in knowledge will arise if this new instrument of cognition can be taken up in an appropriate way.

Rudolf Steiner describes a quite different effect of the phantom, which has been conveyed to all people unconsciously as a fact of life, in relation to human powers of reproduction:

The interplay of ahrimanic and luciferic powers had indeed developed to the extent where, at the time of the Mystery of Golgotha, humanity on earth would actually have died away. And through what occurred at the Mystery of Golgotha ... humanity was healed and prevented from dying out. The human physical body was once again endowed with a vitality enabling human beings to pass through their further evolution on earth in such a way that they can continue to descend from soul-spiritual worlds and retain the capacity to inhabit physical bodies. This was the very real effect of the Mystery of Golgotha.[40]

In this specific context, Rudolf Steiner refers to the lecture cycle *From Jesus to Christ* – that is, to his insight into and description of the phantom – and stresses that one could 'of course express this same fact in many other ways'.[41] This cycle has particular importance in Rudolf Steiner's complete works,

> ... because certain truths which many people wish to remain concealed were expressed here from a sense of esoteric obligation, this attracted a great deal of enmity. One can even say that this cycle was specifically what triggered enmity in certain quarters.[42]

The reason for this enmity is the fact that understanding of the phantom shows the Resurrection to be the source of complete transubstantiation of the human being; in other words, the transformation goes right into physical substance, and does not only affect beliefs and opinions. The very bases for materialism thus fade away.

I have presented all this here because Prokofieff is working with a strangely one-sided and undifferentiated view of the physical body. In the entirety of the physical body lie the most diverse qualities. When Prokofieff quotes Steiner's comment that in relation to the new manifestation of Christ in the etheric body 'His reappearance in a physical body is ruled out',[43] this must relate to the 'old Adam', and certainly not to the 'new Adam'. The same applies to Prokofieff's insistence that preparation for the reappearance of Christ occurs for the human being 'in a pure, that is to say, sense-free way, and not through the forces and impressions of the physical body'.[44]

These physical forces, however, also include those whereby the child builds up his body during the first three years and forms it with the guidance of the higher hierarchies. The wisest person

> ... can therefore learn a great deal from the child, for he can see beyond and through the child in front of him into the world of spirit; for the child has a 'phone connection' to the spiritual world which is later cut off. In the first three years, we therefore have a quite different being before us than we do later. We have a child 'I' that works sculpturally under the guidance of the higher hierarchies at developing and forming the human instruments of thinking. Then this I enters into these instruments, and can no longer work upon them. The human instruments of thinking must already be formed and developed.[45]

The instruments of thinking, the physical brain, therefore grow as it were out of the world of spirit. Once this work is finished, an incisive process of separation occurs in the human being. 'In esoteric parlance one calls the first human being the divine human being, or the son of God, because he is related to the higher hierarchies; the other is called the son of man.[46] Rudolf Steiner makes clear the connection of the divine with the physical nature of the human being:

We sink down into our son of man; the son of God can no longer hold sway over our son of man after three years. Yet we still bear this son of God within us; these forces work within the physical body throughout life, though they can no longer directly participate in building it. If we look into ourselves we can find the continuation of the I that had that 'phone connection'. But now the physical body is too solid, coarse and intransigent for the son of God to continue working sculpturally on it.[47]

In this son of God in the human being we can no doubt see something that has a direct relationship with the phantom, even if this lecture was given before the cycle *From Jesus to Christ*. This view is justified above all by Rudolf Steiner's comment that 'these forces ... also have an upbuilding, health-giving and enlivening quality',[48] and especially by his remark that the adult can transform these forces through spiritual work into forces of healing. If the human being can

> ... fully use [these forces] through esoteric wisdom, then they flow out through his fingertips and he acquires the special gift of healing by laying on of hands – if they are still active, these spiritual forces no longer transform one's own body but instead, when they flow out, exert a blessed and healing effect.[49]

In this way I want to point out that in the highly complex human physical body a wealth of forces are at work which must be clearly differentiated and to which Rudolf Steiner's phrase also applies, that 'To the outward senses, the spirit-permeated physical body indeed appears only sensory in nature.'[50]

Today the modern, incarnated human being is truly a 'mixed king'.[51] Working in him is the karma that he brings with him from his previous incarnations and which – by no means always harmoniously – connects him with genetic forces. In his incarnations after Christ, whether few or many, he may already have developed a connection with the Christ being, and have already begun to transform his supersensible bodies, the spiritual fruits of which work in him and cannot be lost. He is also affected from without by the complex influences of our technological civilization. Thus the human being has become someone in whom work opposing forces which need to be differentiated and examined in detail – as I have tried to do here in relation to stigmatization.

Continuous Fasting

'It is touching and absurd when friendly visitors bring restorative wines, fruits ... and food. Therese has not eaten or drunk since 1926.'[52] These succinct words address an important phenomenon that often – though not always – arises in connection with stigmatization. In the case of Anne Catherine Emmerich, Therese Neumann and Judith von Halle, continuous fasting becomes a condition of life and destiny that arises with stigmatization. Accounts about Saint Francis are unclear in this respect. For those named above – and I will only speak of them here – continuous fasting is simply part of stigmatization: another, perhaps even more incisive aspect of the entire phenomenon, that cannot be separated from it. Both aspects sustain and determine each other. Not eating creates the physical basis for the bleeding, and for healing powers, and naturally also for experiences in special states of awareness.

The astonishing and ultimately incomprehensible thing in Prokofieff's account of stigmatics is that he does not refer to such fasting at all. This is nonsensical for any account or description that claims academic credibility. Because Prokofieff ignores the fact that these stigmatics do not eat, all his comments are inevitably one-sided, and their academic value highly dubious.

In the history of scientific research, the worst method has always been simply to overlook or even deny phenomena that are not easily explicable or which even undermine one's preferred world view. Instead of honestly attending to the problems such phenomena pose for knowledge, and attempting to explore them, they are suppressed. No doubt this is due to a kind of underlying fear that the relevant phenomenon will question all one's assumptions.

Bertolt Brecht gave a fine instance of this in his play *Galileo*. The eponymous hero has trained his telescope on Jupiter and its moons in order to persuade the cardinal that these moons can really be seen. The latter however does not even deign to look through the telescope, saying: 'I don't need to look through the telescope, as I know that these moons of Jupiter do not exist.'

Denying facts still plays a part to this day in accounts of Caspar Hauser, inasmuch as it is disputed that he was incarcerated with only bread and water to sustain him, although this can be proven in diverse ways. In such cases, a materialistic view invariably feels threatened by a phenomenon that seems not to accord with natural laws, which it cannot explain and which it therefore feels compelled to deny.

It is similar with the phenomenon of continuous fasting. Experience has shown that accounts of stigmatization as a psychological rarity meet with some degree of openness and acceptance; but when continuous fasting is mentioned, an abyss of understanding often opens up. Anyone who mentions it finds he loses all credibility. It is indeed a hard test to meet something really extraordinary with an open mind. Even people familiar with anthroposophy and to some extent schooled in spiritual science find the phenomenon of continuous fasting impossible to accept. A frequent objection is that a person's organs would be bound to shrivel up. But this overlooks the fact that continuous fasting is the expression of a comprehensive and utter change to the whole organism, which naturally also includes lymph formation.

The continuous fasting that arises in association with stigmatization is not the result of intentional fasting or an ascetic way of life, but an inherent part of the sudden stroke of destiny. Prior to receiving the stigmata they do not contemplate embarking on such an extraordinary state, and are entirely unaware that it might be possible. The decisive thing in stigmatics' continuous fasting is the *impossibility* of eating, rather than the desire not to eat. The organism responds to attempts to eat food as though to a poison, vehemently rejecting earthly substances.

A particularly astonishing phenomenon in this context is the way these stigmatics put on and lose weight, by amounts ranging from 1 to three kilos – in the case of Therese Neumann sometimes also more – in connection with their experiences each week between Thursday and Sunday.

Continuous fasting poses the question of how the substance of the human body is specifically formed. We know that this happens involuntarily and repeatedly. On the one hand, food is absorbed, but on the other is then very largely broken down and destroyed, and above all robbed of its own characteristics. Thus building up of the body and breakdown of food stand in opposition to each other in a sense. With continuous fasting, the aspect of breaking down is not present, while building up of the body continues for years or decades. In stigmatics who live without eating, the formation of the body occurs as though from nothing. Corporeal substance is created as a special form of matter, for these people still appear as material human beings. Forming and building up of the body from nothing manifests as a corporeal and material phenomenon. Something visible arises from invisibility.

This process occurs as creative act of will in the deepest subconscious of those concerned, and can neither be invoked nor affected by conscious awareness; it manifests as a continuum of life.

Such a continuum cannot be caused by any psychological

Continuous Fasting   39

means, either by auto-suggestion, hysteria or any kind of 'somnambulism'. Psychological states do not reach into the depths where actual corporeal substance is formed. That is why those who study the theme carefully, dismiss the view that stigmatization is caused by auto-suggestion or hysteria.

It is also important to note that by far the greatest problem of not eating is its continuous nature. While the special states of consciousness of stigmatics occur during certain periods of time, not eating is a state that endures through life.

The findings of modern physics and biochemistry can show us that modern science is at least on the way to understanding a phenomenon such as continuous fasting – which was not the case 40 or 50 years ago.

Here of course we need to explore what spiritual science might contribute to an understanding of continuous fasting. It should be unnecessary, though, to point out that we cannot claim to be able to solve one of the greatest problems of knowledge. The scientific and spiritual-scientific research of the future may one day be able to do so, but this does not exclude the possibility that we can draw on available findings to try to understand it today.

Above all we need to examine the relationship that exists between continuous fasting and the phantom that appears in both inner and outer stigmatization. Since stigmatization is a total phenomenon, continuous fasting – as the more immediately corporeal aspect of stigmatization – is also connected with the phantom.

A first step involves becoming aware – or perhaps we should even say admitting – that our current corporeality is an expression of the first, old Adam who was driven out of Paradise. To use an expression coined by Rudolf Steiner that has already been cited above in connection with the human reproductive capacity, we can say: 'The interplay of ahrimanic and luciferic powers had indeed developed to the extent'[53] that it became necessary for the human being, as mortal human being on earth, to have to eat earthly food. This expresses the fact that in the course of evolution the human being connected himself with these ahrimanic and luciferic powers. However, this process is one that draws down or degrades the phantom as archetypal form of the physical body. Rudolf Steiner characterizes this as degeneration:

> We could view this degeneration in a certain sense in terms of the fact that this phantom was really, from the beginnings of human evolution, destined to remain untouched by the material aspects that the human being absorbs as food from the mineral, plant or animal kingdom. It did not remain untouched however, for the luciferic influence gave rise to a close connection between the phantom and the forces which the human being absorbs through earthly evolution – especially the ash constituents.[54]

That our current mode of absorbing food became necessary due to the degeneration of the phantom does not mean that we should look down on such food or even despise it, for it demonstrates only the profound transformation which human nature will have to undergo in order to be able to receive the phantom restored by the Resurrection. It is of course impossible to think that we can receive the phantom without shedding the 'old Adam'.

> And it is possible to create that connection to Christ through which the human being on earth incorporates his otherwise corruptible physical body into this phantom that was resurrected from the grave at Golgotha. It is possible for the human being to receive into his organization those forces which were resurrected then, in the same way as he

received the Adam forces into his physical organization due to luciferic powers at the start of earth evolution.[55]

Not in the field of nutrition but in relation to breathing, Rudolf Steiner described the radical change and indeed the reversal of a process currently natural to us:

> What does breathing signify for occult development? Its significance lies in 'not killing', 'not harming life'. The occult teacher says: You continually kill your surroundings by your breathing ... we breathe in air filled with oxygen, bind it within us with carbon and breathe out carbon dioxide – in which, however, no human being or animal can live. We breathe in oxygen and breathe out a toxic substance, carbon dioxide; in other words, with every breath we kill other beings, gradually killing our whole surroundings.

In our current evolutionary era, it is thanks to plants that toxic carbon dioxide is transformed back again into life-giving oxygen: 'This process will change in future however; and since a person who embarks on esoteric development starts to do what the others will eventually undergo in future, he has to shed the habit of breathing in a way that kills.'[56] Completely reversing the process of breathing through occult schooling is only conceivable by drawing the phantom towards one so that physical human nature gradually unites with its source and archetype – which was raised to a higher level through the Resurrection. We can say this even though Rudolf Steiner had not yet conceived the idea of the phantom in 1906. Above we cited the sentence where he states that 'Through what a human being today can undergo as initiation ... a bond of attraction is created between him' and the phantom. Every spiritual pupil is at some stage on the path of knowledge.

One can also connect with continuous fasting Rudolf Steiner's insight that the law of conservation of energy does not hold true for the human being. He describes this law as

> ... the great obstacle to understanding the human being at all. The moment one thinks that no new energies are ever really created, one will be unable to gain insight into the true nature of the human being. In fact this true human nature consists precisely in the fact that new forces are formed by it continuously. In the context in which we live in the world, the human being is actually the only being in whom new forces and – as we will see later – even new substances are formed.[57]

New creation of forces and substances is the basis of continuous fasting. This process is only conceivable if the phantom works in someone, insofar as this is the physical and spiritual basis of human life. This idea is supported by the fact that the earth is kept alive through the creation of substance as mediating process in the human being:

> What actually occurs in the human being? On the one hand we have the nature that consists of bones and nerves, and on the other the nature consisting of blood and muscles. Through the interplay of both, substances and forces are continually created anew. The earth is preserved from dying by the fact that substances and forces are newly created in the human being.[58]

In the light of this insight into the human being, continuous fasting appears to be a phenomenon that has not yet been fully understood but which belongs intrinsically to human nature as a pointer towards a future transformation.

At the Last Supper, Christ gave His disciples bread and wine, and they received HIM within it, His substance in their substance, so as to transform the whole of human nature. This showed the I the path from the mortal body to the 'incorruptible body': 'His Resurrection is the birth of a new member of human nature: an incorruptible body.'[59] This 'incorruptible body', which is identical with the phantom, brings about the transubstantiation at the Last Supper, by means of which human beings and the earth can begin to overcome earthly nature and liberate themselves from it.

In continuous fasting – as stated above – an aspect that works in all of us is revealed. This is the night or will aspect, through which we are rooted in the world of spirit without usually knowing anything about it. At the same time it is the realm in which the human body is built up and nourished, and in which the higher I has its dwelling, the sphere of the Grail. The Grail is inseparably connected with the Mystery of Golgotha, with the Last Supper, the Crucifixion and Resurrection. In the work by Wolfram von Eschenbach, who was a great Christian initiate, the Grail is portrayed as a stone upon which the phoenix is burned to ash; the ash, here understood as the indestructible aspect of the human being, gives new life to him again, as though in rebirth. We can see this as an indication of the human being's I, which repeatedly incarnates as it evolves. In medieval times a poem or literary work could not yet express this insight directly.

The Grail meal that is often characterized as miraculous nourishment, represents the upbuilding aspect of food in a really wonderfully precise way. In Wolfram's account, the Grail furnishes food and drink individually, appropriate to the I of each recipient: rather than giving one food only, it transforms itself in devotion to the one it wishes to nourish. In a certain sense it relinquishes itself to serve the existence of the one who receives it. In this process, Wolfram describes the forces of formation and preservation of the human body which emanate from the 'incorruptible body'; for what he portrays is nothing other than the reality in which we all live, and the way in which we ceaselessly receive grace.

The Grail stone receives its powers each Good Friday through a dove which brings a small, white wafer – or in other words the strength to furnish on earth everything that once more possesses the perfection of paradise. This is a concealed occurrence in the invisible realm, out of which we are formed and nourished.

The dove which brings the power of heaven once more to the Grail stone each Good Friday can be seen in connection with the wave or current that streams through the earth from the impetus of each Easter Sunday, which we referred to earlier (p. 15).

Seen as the prefiguring of a future condition, continuous fasting is connected in diverse ways with all the powers which emanate from the Mystery of Golgotha. Its appearance in stigmatics is a sign of the real intervention of Christ in earthly evolution, through the Resurrection, of the creation of the phantom and the 'incorruptible body'.

Normative Morals

As a Jew, Richard Pollak intentionally sacrificed himself to share in the fate of the Jewish people, and died at Birkenau in 1943. It is therefore of course an extremely sensitive issue to engage with Prokofieff where he cites Richard Pollak as an example of the right way to approach stigmatization. A sacrifice of this kind unquestionably deserves the highest respect and the profoundest admiration. Nevertheless it has to be said that Prokofieff only cites Richard Pollak in order as it were to invoke a moral authority beyond dispute. In this sense Prokofieff appears to *use* Richard Pollak.

It is part of Richard Pollak's biography that – before he became personally acquainted with Rudolf Steiner in 1907 – the stigmata had appeared on him in the course of a mystical path of Christian schooling. This corresponds precisely with what Rudolf Steiner described in the above-quoted passage from the lecture cycle *From Jesus to Christ*. In her biographical portrait of Pollak, Elisabeth Bessau writes: 'In severe battles of the soul, he eventually found that this path cannot accord with the requirements of our time.'[60] Prokofieff quotes Hilde Pollak as follows: 'Richard had in this incarnation indeed taken on a Jewish bodily organism, but several decades ago the wounds of Christ appeared on his body, thus showing where he belonged as regards his inner nature. Nevertheless, he kept these phenomena hidden as far as possible.'[61] These words by his wife show clearly that the appearance of the stigmata was a result of Richard Pollak's path of schooling, for then one would expect, at least, that they could remain hidden. That Prokofieff cites Richard Pollak as witness for the proper way of dealing with the stigmata indicates once again that he appears to be unaware of the clear distinction between stigmatization acquired on the path of schooling or arising suddenly and involuntarily as a stroke of destiny. Only the acquired stigmata can really be concealed. Prokofieff cites Rudolf Steiner in support of his view: 'As Richard Pollak was the only stigmatic who was closely connected with Rudolf Steiner, it is obvious that he must have discussed the phenomenon with him.'[62] This statement is pure speculation on the part of Prokofieff, for there is no evidence to show in what way the stigmata still appeared on Richard Pollak, having arisen on the path of schooling he had long since abandoned, nor is there any record of conversations which Steiner is supposed to have had with Pollak on this subject. Naturally Prokofieff assumes that Rudolf Steiner confirmed Richard Pollak in his decision to conceal these marks; yet the latter had made this decision himself years before – and it is one easily understood and worthy of respect.

As the following sentence shows, however, Prokofieff is ultimately more concerned with something else: 'However, what is most deeply stirring about Richard Pollak's destiny are not his stigmata but the moral greatness and true Christlike quality which this man showed in later years.'[63] This intends to suggest that the stigmata do not necessarily have anything to do with moral grandeur and truly Christian virtues; for Prokofieff, however, the right way to approach stigmatization, and the ethical qualities he refers to, merge in an especially exemplary moral figure. Since the whole appendix of his book is nothing other than a dispute with the stigmatic Judith von Halle, Sergei Prokofieff's moral message to Judith von Halle is simple: she should have acted as exemplified by the great moral example of Richard Pollak! In this case, her moral elevation would have been certain; but now – compared with this other exemplary figure – it is not even necessary to utter the self-evident moral verdict. This is Prokofieff's method of leading the reader almost unnoticed to the judgement he wishes to invoke.

The first thing to be said is that there is very little in common between Richard Pollak and Judith von Halle, but instead quite extreme differences: from the different nature of their stigmatization through the different conditions of their times to differences of education, profession and work. The example can hardly act as example, therefore, where so few similarities of destiny exist.

Secondly, we need to be aware that Prokofieff here sets up a moral norm with the aim of showing that another individual does not fulfil it. This is the very opposite of the ethical individualism which Steiner's *Philosophy of Freedom* seeks to educate in us. Establishing a moral norm is to fall back into the realm of 'categorical imperative'. How could an author who wrote a book entitled *Anthroposophy and the Philosophy of Freedom* take this same philosophical work by Steiner so little to heart, and, above all, apply it so little?

The individuality and destiny of Judith von Halle need to be evaluated, instead, in an individual way.

Supposed Authorities

At the end of his appendix, Prokofieff cites two anthroposophical authorities – Ita Wegman and Carl Unger – in order as it were to call expert witnesses to support his views. Why should this be necessary if his account is persuasive and conclusive? Isn't this an expression of the uncertainty of an author who suddenly senses that his readers might notice the weaknesses and errors in his argument? Relying on authorities is, at least, not appropriate in a research context.

The chief question to be asked here is whether these two people – who are indeed authorities in diverse fields – can be seen as having anything authoritative to say on stigmatization. Both the statements quoted by Prokofieff were made very soon after Therese Neumann of Konnersreuth received the stigmata. In other words, due to the lack of intervening time, they were writing without any closer knowledge of the phenomena – many of which only became known years later. The account by Carl Unger may be inwardly consistent, but Prokofieff does not appreciate that it may not actually be applicable to the reality of stigmatization. It is certainly questionable whether and what 'pathological loosening of the supersensible bodies' applied in her case, and whether a spiritual-scientific explanation of stigmatization is really offered by suggesting that 'spiritual facts that cannot be psychologically integrated' sink down in the human organization through the bodily sheaths into the physical body. Above all it is unclear what Carl Unger means by saying that 'a counter-image of initiation processes is created'. In what way do stigmatics offer such a counter-image? With all respect for the achievements and person of Carl Unger, whom Rudolf Steiner greatly esteemed, his account suffers from the same problems as the whole of Prokofieff's appendix: no attention is paid to actual observations, and the circumstances and phenomena themselves are scarcely considered, if at all. In these statements by Carl Unger, for instance, no mention is made of continuous fasting, perhaps because this was not yet known of in 1927; yet it is not possible to comment fully on stigmatization without considering continuous fasting. Every anthroposophical account can be evaluated by determining the extent to which it achieves an accord between perception and thinking. In this case this cannot be established, as too few observations were available, but also, primarily, because the thought process presented is a closed circle.

This is also true to some extent of Ita Wegman's article entitled 'How should a medicine oriented to spiritual science regard phenomena such as those at Konnersreuth?'[64] It is simply untrue of Prokofieff to say that Ita Wegman wrote her article 'after a thorough investigation of the available facts'.[65] This 'thorough investigation' was impossible simply because the 'facts' were not yet known in 1927 when she wrote her article. Only from the 30s onwards were observations recorded which, for Wegman too, could have substantially altered the picture. Ita Wegman sent her assistant Dr Schickler to Konnersreuth to witness her at first hand and report back. It is beyond dispute that involuntary stigmatization is not a path of knowledge and cannot be achieved by any psychic or psychological efforts. Nevertheless, Ita Wegman showed a quite different kind of understanding for the extraordinary phenomenon of Therese Neumann's stigmatization than Prokofieff, who harnesses Wegman to his argument in a one-sided way by withholding important comments of hers. In the introduction to her article, Wegman writes:

> The facts preoccupying all minds at present, which are unfolding in Konnersreuth, have led me to try to illumine them from the perspectives of spiritual-scientific medicine. These events, that seem like a miracle, strike one as an invitation to concern oneself with supersensible realities. We must acknowledge that this surely has a deeper meaning for us as something that demands our attention. I recall a conversation I once had with Rudolf Steiner in which he spoke of the significant events that occurred at Caspar Hauser's mysterious appearance, which also greatly preoccupied the world at that time. He pointed out that the key thing about such mysterious events lay precisely in the fact that all minds were thereby compelled to attend to something most unusual that could not be understood by resorting to a mundane view of things. It was an attempt by the world of spirit, he said, to remind people, in the midst of a largely materialistic age, that there are more things in heaven and earth than philistine thinking could even dream of. Thus, from time to time, such events occur that strike one as miraculous, and which can only be understood through a knowledge of the world of spirit. Because they seem so hard to explain, they preoccupy everyone and remind people again of the reality of the spirit.[66]

A quite different stance and attitude speaks from these words by Ita Wegman about Therese Neumann's stigmatization than the view put forward by Prokofieff. Through her conversation with Rudolf Steiner, Wegman is aware that an event such as stigmatization is only conceivable through the will of the world of spirit. By ignoring this vital comment by Wegman, Prokofieff not only argues one-sidedly, but also tries to make it seem as if Ita Wegman, as a great anthroposophical

Supposed Authorities 51

authority, shares his view of stigmatization. This is also how he uses Carl Unger's account. With all respect for the two anthroposophical authorities Prokofieff draws on for his purposes, a sober appraisal shows them not to be authoritative on the matter of stigmatization. Their warning against false paths into the spiritual world, and their accentuation of conscious and voluntary schooling through spiritual science, miss the point here. Prokofieff's whole account is repeatedly burdened by his basic error in relation to the real nature of stigmatization as it manifests in the stigmatics cited here.

At the conclusion of his comments in the appendix, Prokofieff goes so far as to use the 'verdicts, founded on spiritual science, of these two important pupils and colleagues of Rudolf Steiner' – which as we have seen cannot be related to Prokofieff's views on stigmatization – as authoritative support for his opinions. Still worse, in his final sentence he claims that, as pupils of Rudolf Steiner, these two authorities would have been 'completely in harmony with his intentions'.[67] In other words, Rudolf Steiner is by this means enlisted to support Prokofieff's opinions. This is nothing other than enormous presumption.

Afterword

The phrase 'resurrection body' used by Prokofieff needs some clarification. Firstly, Rudolf Steiner never used this word – it does not appear anywhere in his Collected Works (GA). In the lecture cycle *From Jesus to Christ* Rudolf Steiner used the word 'phantom' as a kind of technical term, and from then on used it consistently except where he spoke more indirectly about what the word 'phantom' refers to, as is the case in the quotation given earlier from *The Study of Man*. There he describes how the I works on the child as the submerged son of God, and how the capacity of human reproduction is acquired and preserved through the phantom.

Many readers of Rudolf Steiner's works have found difficulty with this word 'phantom'. This is comprehensible since, after nearly a hundred years, the word is only really used in contexts that have nothing to do with the meaning Rudolf Steiner gives it.[68] It is therefore understandable that the phrase 'resurrection body' was coined, and is widely used. It is not easy to find out who first used it, and this hardly matters. It must be stressed, however, that this expression naturally can apply only to the phantom *after* the Resurrection, and that Rudolf Steiner did not make this distinction between phantom and resurrection body.

But right at the beginning of his book, Prokofieff speaks of the 'fashioning of the Resurrection body'[69] without – as he always otherwise does – citing a source in Rudolf Steiner's works or drawing attention to its problematic nature. Prokofieff is certainly not concerned to use a better-sounding phrase, but instead also connects this phrase with his view of stigmatization. This is clear from his words at the beginning of the appendix. Stigmatization, he says, 'has in itself no relationship to the phantom', and justifies this statement by saying: 'For the bleeding wounds on the physical body form part of what happened *before* the Resurrection. After the Resurrection, the phantom was no longer imbued with any material substance.'[70] Prokofieff thus seeks to back up his thesis by claiming that stigmatization has nothing to do with the Resurrection, but instead with the state of suffering prior to it, which is overcome with the Resurrection. But through the Resurrection the stigmata are absorbed into the phantom and even serve Christ, when He appears on several occasions, as confirmation of His Resurrection. They belong to the phantom as 'form of the human figure which, as a spiritual fabric, processes the physical substances and forces in such a way that they assume the shape we see as human being on the physical plane'.[71] Prokofieff also calls the wound marks 'points of densification on the etheric body of the Risen One', which cannot give rise to any 'material effect'.[72] What this is intended to mean can only be understood in the light of Prokofieff's efforts to discredit stigmatization as a material phenomenon. Both the phantom and also the invisible etheric body – which is after all a causal influence on the life functions of the body – shape and work into the bodily sheaths and produce physical, material phenomena. A division really does not exist. The invisible becomes visible.

Through an overview and comparison of related comments by Rudolf Steiner in the cycle *From Jesus to Christ*, I want to try to get closer to the concept which Steiner terms 'the phantom'. This concept is multi-layered and diverse, and above all alive. It is no doubt the richest and thus most complex and difficult concept that there is.

Rudolf Steiner starts with Paul, who distinguished between the first (also called 'old') and the second ('new') Adam, the latter being identical with Christ:

Paul regards the second Adam, the Christ in contrast [to the first] as indwelling the incorruptible and immortal body. Paul assumes that through Christian evolution human beings will gradually become able, in place of the first Adam, to draw to themselves, or clothe themselves in the incorruptible body of the second Adam.[73]

In the second Adam, through Christ, a spiritual archetype is created to which all people can relate through their I if they wish to become Christians: 'You can likewise draw spiritual connections from what lives in you, in this way, to a second Adam, to Christ, and indeed to that Christ who rose from the grave on the third day.'[74]

The next step is the introduction of the word 'phantom' as the 'form of the human figure' that is here also described as 'the real idea in the outer world'.[75] This synonym for 'phantom' can greatly aid our understanding, as it refers to the sphere from which the effects derive.

The phantom is the form of the physical body into which the luciferic influences entered as substance and matter evolved, making this body visible and mortal. Through these influences, the phantom of the physical human body was gradually destroyed. The germ of this phantom was created on Old Saturn by the Thrones, and evolved through Old Sun and Moon stages until the Earth embodiment. Thus it is a lofty and complex configuration.

From the grave at Golgotha arose the 'pure phantom of the physical human being – bearing the forces of its physical and material parts – with all properties of the physical body'.[76] By this means it became possible for the human being 'to establish the relationship with Christ which enables the earthly human being to incorporate this phantom, resurrected from the grave at Golgotha, into his otherwise corruptible physical body.'[77] The word 'incorporate' characterizes the process that was described above in terms of the 'mixed king'.

The fact that this human phantom 'could be saved in the passage through death' led to the creation of a new sheath or member within the entirety of the human being: 'His Resurrection is the birth of a new member of human nature, of an incorruptible body.'[78] The expression 'incorruptible body', in close proximity and connection with the phantom, is the closest Steiner comes to the phrase 'resurrection body'.

The whole fluidity of the concept as Steiner presents it becomes fully apparent when the 'incorruptible body' is placed into another context:

> But the event of Golgotha occurred, and brought about a complete redress of the human being's lost evolutionary principles. By taking up what we yesterday named as the 'incorruptible body'... by incorporating this incorruptible body into him, he will increasingly render his I consciousness ever brighter, will increasingly perceive within his nature what passes from one incarnation to the next.[79]

Between the 'birth' and the 'redress' exists a lively tension which is necessary for understanding the phantom.

A further perspective arises from the fact that

> ...when this body of Jesus of Nazareth was nailed to the Cross, the phantom was actually entirely intact, existing as the spiritual-physical but only supersensibly visible form, and was in a much looser connection with the material content than in any other human being.[80]

This shows the exceptional situation of the God Christ, as human being, as opposed to all other human beings.

Rudolf Steiner also describes the phantom 'on which

depends the evolution of the I'[81] as the 'spirit body'[82] which Mary Magdalene, the disciples and Paul were able to perceive. This 'spirit body', a synonym for the phantom, also however has the capacity to become visible and tangible to sensory experience, as no doubt first happened on the way to Emmaus.

The phantom created during Old Saturn is the form of the physical body, the real idea in the external world; the spirit body, in which the lost evolutionary principles of the first Adam were redressed, gives rise to the second Adam. With the incorruptible body a new member or sheath of the human being is born. Christ Himself is the bearer of the pure phantom.

Prokofieff does not explore this extraordinary multiplicity of the phantom in his account. There are two main reasons for this. Firstly, the gradual attraction, investiture and incorporation of the phantom and its gradual assimilation into the physical body, is alien to him. This is concealed in the visible and material realm, but can also certainly be perceived. Understanding spiritual science requires a certain relationship to the phantom, a first, partial receptiveness to and absorption of it.

Secondly, Prokofieff regards stigmatization as a retrograde step that refers back to the phantom before the Resurrection. Quite apart from whether this view has any justification at all, it can only be proposed by ignoring the decisive phenomenon of continuous fasting, as explained above. For Prokofieff, without further careful differentiation, all corporeal and material phenomena are intrinsically suspicious through their relation to the old Adam.

Prokofieff also tries to enlist Rudolf Steiner to support his view of stigmatization through the way he presents the 'resurrection body'. This is clear from the fact that he

Afterword   57

repeatedly cites Rudolf Steiner whenever he refers to the resurrection body.[83] The message is clear: Rudolf Steiner has a connection with the resurrection body, but Judith von Halle does not.

Notes

(Quotations from Rudolf Steiner have been translated directly from the German originals. For a list of published English translations see the list on p. 63.)

1. Sergei O. Prokofieff: *Das Mysterium der Auferstehung im Lichte der Anthroposophie*, Verlag Freies Geistesleben, Stuttgart 2008. English edition: *The Mystery of the Resurrection in the Light of Anthroposophy*, Temple Lodge Publishing, Sussex 2010.
2. In the English edition of the book (see above) the author adds an Addendum in which he openly refers to Judith von Halle.
3. Translator's note: The use of the nobility designation 'von' for Emmerich is certainly false.
4. *The Mystery of the Resurrection*, p. 133.
5. Rudolf Steiner: *The Philosophy of Freedom*, GA 4, in the chapter 'Thinking in the Service of Knowledge': The content of sensation, perception and contemplation, all feelings, acts of will, dreams and fancies, mental pictures, concepts and ideas, all illusions and hallucinations, are given to us through observation. (Michael Wilson translation.) See also the chapter 'The World as Percept'.
6. Prokofieff, op. cit., p. 148.
7. Translator's note: this is no doubt also the root of the double meaning of the word 'stigmatized' in English.
8. Judith von Halle: *And If He Has Not Been Raised...* Temple Lodge Publishing 2007, p. 69.
9. Rudolf Steiner: *Ursprungsimpulse der Geisteswissenschaft*, GA 96, Dornach 2005, p. 82.
10. Ibid, p. 289.
11. Ibid, p. 295.
12. Luise Rinser: *Die Wahrheit über Konnersreuth*, Frankfurt am Main 1954, p. 133.

13. W. Garvelmann: *Sie sehen Christus*, Verlag am Goetheanum, Dornach 2008, p. 43 ff.
14. Rudolf Steiner: *Die Geheimwissenschaft im Umriss*, GA 13 Dornach 1977, p. 143.
15. Prokofieff, op. cit., p. 147.
16. Cf. in this connection Judith von Halle: 'Vom Mysterium des Kreuzsymbols', Newsletter of the Humanities Section, Dornach, Winter/spring 2008/09, no. 3.
17. Prokofieff, op. cit., p. 151.
18. L. Rinser, op. cit., p. 130.
19. Rudolf Steiner: *Das Markus-Evangelium*, GA 139, Dornach 1976, p. 188.
20. Prokofieff, op. cit., p. 144 f.
21. Ibid, p. 145.
22. L. Rinser, op. cit., p. 153 f.
23. Ibid, p. 151.
24. Ibid, p. 153.
25. Ibid, p. 155.
26. Ibid, p. 78.
27. Prokofieff, op. cit., p. 141.
28. Ibid.
29. Ibid.
30. Henry Thode: *Franz von Assisi und die Anfänge der Kunst der Renaissance in Italien*, first edition 1885, popular edition 1934.
31. Ibid, p. 758.
32. Ibid, p. 773.
33. Ibid, p. 774.
34. Ibid, p. 775.
35. Ibid, p. 775 f.
36. Ibid, p. 776.
37. Ibid, p. 775.
38. Rudolf Steiner: *Von Jesus zu Christus*, GA 131, Dornach 1974, p. 212 f.
39. Ibid, p. 214.
40. Rudolf Steiner, 7 May 1923: *Die menschliche Seele in ihrem*

Zusammenhang mit göttlich-geistigen Individualitäten, GA 224, Dornach 1983, p. 148.
41. Ibid, p. 149.
42. Ibid, p. 148 f.
43. Prokofieff, op. cit., p. 165.
44. Ibid, p. 166.
45. Rudolf Steiner, Zurich, 25 February 1911: *Die Mission der neuen Geistesoffenbarung*, GA 127, p. 88f.
46. Ibid, p. 89.
47. Ibid, p. 90.
48. Ibid, p. 89.
49. Ibid, p. 91.
50. Rudolf Steiner: *Theosophie*, GA 9, 1948 edition, p. 64.
51. A reference to the 'mixed king' in Goethe's fairy tale of 'The Green Snake and the Beautiful Lily'.
52. L. Rinser, op. cit., p. 109.
53. Rudolf Steiner, 7 May 1923: *Die menschliche Seele in ihrem Zusammenhang mit göttlich-geistigen Individualitäten*, GA 224, Dornach 1983, p. 148.
54. Rudolf Steiner: *Von Jesus zu Christ*, GA 131, Dornach 1974, p. 185.
55. Ibid, p. 167.
56. Rudolf Steiner: *Vor dem Tore der Theosophie*, GA 95, Dornach 1978, p. 122f.
57. Rudolf Steiner: *Allgemeine Menschenkunde als Grundlage der Pädagogik*, GA 293, Dornach 1973, p. 47.
58. Ibid, p. 60.
59. GA 131, p. 171.
60. Bodo von Plato: *Anthroposophie im 20. Jahrhundert*, Dornach 2003, p. 606. Biographical portrait by Elisabeth Bessau.
61. Prokofieff, op. cit., p. 138.
62. Ibid, p. 138.
63. Ibid, p. 138.
64. Ita Wegman: 'Wie bewertet geisteswissenschaftlich orientierte Medizin Erscheinungen wie die in Konnersreuth?' in: *Im*

Anbruch des Wirkens für eine Erweiterung der Heilkunst (articles and essays), Arlesheim 1974, p. 102 ff.
65. Prokofieff, op. cit., p. 167.
66. Wegman, op. cit., p. 102.
67. Prokofieff, op. cit., p. 167.
68. Translator's note: A poem by S. T. Coleridge, entitled 'Phantom' still retains something much closer to Steiner's meaning. Here it is:
All look and likeness caught from earth,
All accident of kin and birth,
Had pass'd away. There was no trace
Of aught on that illumined face,
Upraised beneath the rifted stone
But of one spirit all her own –
She, she herself, and only she,
Shone through her body visibly.
69. Prokofieff, op. cit., p. 3.
70. Ibid, p. 133.
71. Rudolf Steiner: *Von Jesus zu Christus*, GA 131, p. 150.
72. Prokofieff, op. cit., p. 133.
73. Rudolf Steiner: *Von Jesus zu Christus*, GA 131, p. 143.
74. Ibid, p. 145.
75. Ibid, p. 150.
76. Ibid, p. 167.
77. Ibid.
78. Ibid, p. 171.
79. Ibid, p. 170.
80. Ibid, p. 187.
81. Ibid, p. 187.
82. Ibid, pp. 186 and 7.
83. Cf. Prokofieff, op. cit., p. 154 f.

Bibliography of books by Rudolf Steiner

GA (Gesamtausgabe or Collected Works)
-   4   *The Philosophy of Spiritual Activity*
-   9   *Theosophy*
- 13   *Occult Science*
- 95   *Founding a Science of the Spirit*
- 96   *Original Impulse for the Science of the Spirit*
- 127   *Die Mission der neuen Geistesoffenbarung* (not translated)
- 131   *From Jesus to Christ*
- 139   *The Gospel of St. Mark*
- 224   *Die menschliche Seele in ihrem Zusammenhang mit göttlichgeistigen Individualitäten* (not translated)
- 293   *The Study of Man*

English titles available from Rudolf Steiner Press, UK, *www.rudolfsteinerpress.com* or SteinerBooks, USA, *www.steinerbooks.org*

Also available from Temple Lodge Publishing:

Judith von Halle

AND IF HE HAD NOT BEEN RAISED...
The Stations of Christ's Path to Spirit Man
192pp + 3pp colour plates; £14.95;
ISBN 9781902636887

SECRETS OF THE STATIONS OF THE CROSS AND THE GRAIL BLOOD
The Mystery of Transformation
160pp + 4pp colour plates; £11.95;
ISBN 9781902636894

THE LORD'S PRAYER
The Living Word of God
96pp; £9.95; ISBN 9781902636856

ILLNESS AND HEALING
and the Mystery Language of the Gospels
200pp + 4pp colour plates; £12.95;
ISBN 9781902636986